BULLETPROOF HOME SECURITY SYSTEM

D0559100

BULLETPROOF HOME SECURITY SYSTEM

BY FRANK MITCHELL

FAMILY SURVIVAL

ALWAYS SAFE, ALWAYS PREPARED

Printed in the United States of America

First Printing, 2016

ISBN 978-0-9974376-2-1

5280 Publishing, LLC dba FamilySurvival.com
453 E. Wonderview Ave.
Estes Park, CO 80517
www.FamilySurvival.com

DISCLAIMER OF LIABILITY AND WARRANTY

COPYRIGHT

TERMS AND DISCLAIMER

Table Of Contents

Introduction

We are fortunate to live in America, where our cities are relatively safe. Even the worst neighborhoods in our most violent cities don't compare to some other locales across the globe, where mere existence takes effort. Still, we are seeing a remarkable increase in violent crime perpetrated on suburban homes. Once the domain of simple burglaries, the average American home is far more prone to home invasion than it was in the past. Additionally, SWAT team raids are becoming more common; they are alarmingly perpetrated on the *wrong home* with increasing frequency.

THE CRUX OF THE PROBLEM

We don't live in fortified castles, nor is it in vogue to have overt security measures on our homes. Sure, the homes of the wealthy can have a wall and a gate, but what do you think of a neighborhood when you drive by and each home has bars on the windows and steel entry gates on the front door? Easy – you think bad neighborhood, and that's not the image we want to send as preppers. In *bad neighborhoods*, most everyone has the same security measures. In normal, suburban neighborhoods, the house with the gate and barred windows stands out like a sore thumb. As preppers, blending in is part of the deal. Attracting undue attention to your home is not where we want to be, fundamentally. The crux is simple – the home must be fortified to withstand common attacks, but it must not seem visibly fortified.

At this point, many people ask about alarm systems. America has overwhelmingly turned to alarm systems in a quest for home protection. The basic premise is that upon making entry, an alarm will sound (could be a silent one), and a dispatch center will receive the signal. They in turn will notify the police and thus a patrol car will be sent out. Some alarm systems take this a step further by monitoring each window and door, and thus telling the homeowner and transmitting to the alarm company where the break is occurring. Some alarm calls are responded to by the security company's own personnel, which sometimes provide a quicker response within places like gated communities. Alarm systems, however, are not a substitute for home hardening. Here are some reasons why:

- An alarm system does nothing to actually harden the home. The only thing that will potentially deter a hostile person is an 8" placard announcing that the home is protected by an alarm system – *if he or she sees it.*

- Response to an alarm call is considered a nuisance call for most police departments, since hundreds of thousands of false calls happen every year. Sure, they must come out, but they aren't usually in a great hurry.

- If an attacker wants to get in the home, the alarm system won't stop them, and in most parts of the country, an attacker would have over five minutes to loot the home or *harm you.*

- During a natural disaster, your home noisemaker (aka alarm) will most likely be ignored.

As preppers, the last point is the hardest pill to swallow. During a disaster, with first responder resources stretched to the max, a response to an alarm call will basically be the last priority.

Hardening Your Home

It has been said that many medieval castles more or less defended them-selves. The walls alone, due to sheer mass, were enough to keep most skir-mishers outside the gates. Skirmishers were one thing, but a determined force of attackers was quite another. In order to defend the castle against a determined aggressor, *manpower* was needed; the walls were not enough. So too, your home needs *you* to protect it during a time of disaster. You need to be able to maintain the integrity of the home – namely the doors and windows – so that you can keep the attackers out – but in your sights. Once the home's integrity is breached, the battle happens inside, and that is no place to fight at all. Keep people out, and stand a chance. Let people in, and potentially die within your own home. Here are some basic pre-cepts of home hardening:

- No home is impregnable against a determined attacker, but you can slow the entry enough and make the attacker pay dearly enough that he may cease the attack.

- The number one target of break-ins and home invasions (85%) is the front door. Most SWAT teams will conduct operations against the front door as well. Consider that most American door locks (even deadbolts) will survive, on average, two swift kicks, or one hit with a purpose built SWAT style battering ram (manned by one person).

- The weakest exterior door in the home becomes the weakest link in the chain. A super fortified front door can sometimes be located ten feet from an unlocked garage or side door. Make sure you cover all doors!

The bottom line is this – both home invaders and SWAT teams alike use a single element that allows them to succeed – *surprise*. A rapid hit that disables your door and lets an attacker in is a surprise. A window hit that shatters a window backed up by a ladder whereby attackers can pour in is a surprise. *A hit on your front door that does not result in the door opening, however, is a warning* – to you. It's a warning to you to prepare yourself, to get armed. Most importantly, such a failed non-entry is liable to stop an attack in its tracks.

What you need to do to harden your home is to pluck all the low hanging security fruit from your home. You need to harden it enough to deter an invader, make it so his element of surprise is defeated, giving you time to prepare a counterattack. We'll show you how.

The Front Door, and Other Entry Doors

Front doors have been universally accepted in American culture as the place of entry used by visitors, strangers, salesmen, and occasionally, the owners of the home. You must first realize that the only reason this door is used as such is purely cultural. If you don't believe us, try visiting your friend, and knock on the back door. You will most

likely find a rear entry gate wide open, and the back door may even be unlocked – *all signals that it is okay to enter that way.* Yet, your entry at the back door might result in the homeowner calling the police, in the worst case – even though the path was easy to get to. In a sense, the front door is a purely symbolic gateway, yet the door that most often has the highest level of protection – or what passes for protection. Usually, your front door will have the following protective devices:

A DEADBOLT

This is where all the money goes; a lock with a 1 ½" hardened metal rod that protrudes from the door either into the doorframe or the dead side of a double door. The problem with a deadbolt is that even the slightest warpage of the doorframe by a hit can totally defeat it. Additionally, it normally slides into a thin pocket; there simply isn't much meat here.

A CHAIN

This is sometimes used to allow the owner to open the door a crack to speak with someone. The theory here is that the chain will prevent someone from bumping the door open. Often, it's mounted to both sides of the door with short screws and the chain is brass rather than hardened steel.

*None of the methods above are adequate for **any** of your exterior doors.* Here are some solutions that are guaranteed to defeat a first hit entry while being totally invisible from the outside:

DOOR BARRICADE

In use since the medieval times and even before, a simple door barricade can be purchased or even made. It's important that the brackets that hold the crossbeam be lag bolted into the door studs for maximum strength.

Once the crossbeam is bolted into place, there's no amount of pounding on the door that will cause it to budge. An attack on the deadbolt will fail, as will an attack on the hinges -a barricade simply takes the door's weakest parts out of play. In case the wife is cringing, they don't all have  to be ugly – there is no reason why the brackets can't be made of chromed steel and the barricade itself from varnished hardwood.

DOOR STOP

If the door barricade seems a bit much (it's not, trust us), but you live in an apartment, or a temporary dwelling of some sort, consider a door stop made by the Nightlock company. Available most

anywhere on the Internet for $60 or less, and with an installation time in minutes, the Nightlock is a good alternative to a door barricade. While it does allow the top part of the door to flex a bit, it will most certainly deter a one hit bump, especially if you use good hardware to mount it to the floor.

BARREL BOLTS

Barrel bolts don't have to be ugly – and every exterior door (yes, even the one that leads to the garage) should have one. The key here is that the bolt needs to engage directly into the concrete slab or other structural material. It functions very much like the door stop but is excellent for doors where you don't want the look of a door stop. Again, they totally take the air out of a first hit bump and leave the invader wondering just what is holding that door shut – even though he may have the deadbolt in his hand!

Patio Doors

The bane of home security is the humble sliding patio door, which is ubiquitous throughout America. Easily defeated by most crooks since it has a simple hook for locking, this door is easy to jimmy, and with older models, it can be lifted clear off its frame by anyone who has had three minutes of training doing it.

Don't even bother with locks on these guys – go straight to a professional grade patio doorstop. Note we did not say put a broom handle in the track! What you want is for the stop to be engaged midway up the door, about the same level as the lock itself. This is because on a track with old or worn track wheels, an expert can tilt the door

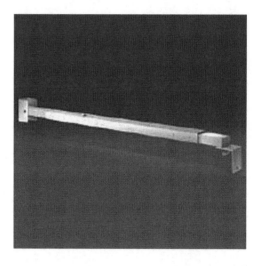

enough, even with a broom handle in place, to cause the door to come off its track or insert a jimmy tool in the gap and pry the door off. Even proper security bars like the one we are suggesting is nothing new, and since patio doors are inherently unsecure virtually no matter what is done to them, consider adding a vertical barrel bolt to the vertical door frame as well to keep the door locked in place.

Nowadays, most patio doors are made of vinyl or some other form of plastic. Aluminum is rare, but out there. However, both will take to drilling just fine. In the event of a real emergency when you can't locate a suitable beam to block the door, simply screw the door shut using common drywall screws. This method won't withstand a determined attack, but it will force an opportunist to try his luck elsewhere on the premises.

Glass – An Intruder's Dream

American homes are covered in glass – there's not much that can be done about it. Formerly reserved for windows, now most American doors have windowpanes; they are obviously present in sliding patio doors as well as some garage doors. Glass is simply a fact of life, and to be honest, one does not necessarily want to live in a windowless hut. Glass has a tendency to defeat other hardening measures as well. For example, you might have a French door that you've installed vertical barrel bolts on. There might even be a cross bar behind the door – but guess what – all a crook needs to do is smash out one little pane of glass, and he can then lift the cross bar off and pull up the barrel bolts. Pretty disappointing – but we have a remedy.

Ballistic window film is the answer here, and it should be installed on your sensitive windows – all your windows if you can afford it. Marketed by a variety of companies, but most prominently adhesives giant 3M, ballistic window film is normally comprised of multiple thin layers of film that are bonded together, then bonded to the window frame of your home. When 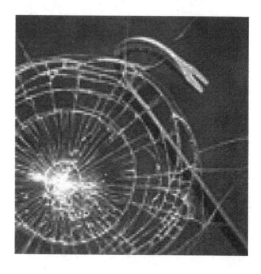 the windows are struck by an object, the glass still shatters – but it all hangs in one piece! The film will not allow the glass to be penetrated, and it will still be in the way as a barrier. It is a remarkably durable and tenacious product that cannot be easily defeated.

3M markets their film under the Ultra Prestige (28 layers of microfilm) and Ultra series (42 layers of microfilm), and while it is relatively expensive and really ought to be installed by a professional, it is worth every penny if you have lots of windows, or windows that are in a bad strategic area, like sidelights on the front door. 3M's marketing literature claims that "windows can be transformed from your weakest link to a source of strength", and they are entirely right on that note. Keep in mind the word "ballistic" does not imply that the film is bulletproof – it is resistant to blunt impacts like bats, bricks, pipes, crowbars, and things of that nature.

Since this guide was originally published, we have fielded hundreds of questions about this film, mainly related to the installation thereof. Let's be right up front with the install – you definitely want a pro to install this. There is one really simple reason why – if the film is installed incorrectly or by someone that hasn't installed ballistic film before, the results will be a hazy, bubbly pane of glass that reduces your ability to *see* the enemy, even if it is still protecting you. Think about it for a minute – you still need situational awareness to be able to defend yourself. Don't shortchange yourself by obscuring your view outside.

A Hidden Access Area No One Thinks About

So you've barricaded all exterior doors, and put 3M window films on your windows for a complete home solution. You feel pretty safe inside your home, but you're missing one huge hole – your *attic vent*. Most American homes are designed on the principle of having a vented attic, which means that the dwelling itself is sealed, but the attic is open to vent to

the outside. Basically, all one needs to do is put a ladder up to the attic vent, unscrew the panel, climb inside, and enter through your attic access. No locks, no broken windows – nothing – *and you might not even know the intruder had even been inside.* Most attic vents are fully capable of fitting a grown man, and most homes have at least one, and sometimes more. Again, our culture has taught us "that's not a door" so most people overlook it as a method of ingress into the home – except crooks. Ask yourself what's protecting the attic access to your home from the inside? Is it a piece of sheetrock painted to match the ceiling just sitting in place by gravity? Is it a lockable door? Could a crook literally walk into your home with nothing but a ladder and a Philips screwdriver, defeating every security measure you have?

The easiest way to kill this one is to have a steel grate or bars made for this vent, and to bolt the grate over the attic vent. Make sure to use through bolts so that the grate cannot be easily removed. Don't worry too much about the look – most attic vents don't face the street and the grate can be painted to match the home.

Skylights – Death From Above

Okay, so 'death from above' is a bit much, but consider that skylights are usually thin plexiglass and more than large enough to fit an intruder. Sure, they may have primitive locks, but they can easily be smashed, drilled, or cut for entry. Most of them are yellowed from the sun, and sunlight breaks down the polycarbonate in the skylight lens, making it brittle and easily fractured. Heck, lots of them crack on their own without any human intervention. The easiest solution here is either a set of bars on the inside, preventing ingress, or the aforementioned 3M films.

Of course we may need to state the obvious here – if you leave the home, don't leave the skylight open! Many skylights tilt to open, leaving a gap of a foot or more. They are hinged units that can easily be forced open, allowing a grown man through without even breaking anything. Make sure your skylights are locked when you are away or sleeping at night.

The Garage Door

Most roll up garage doors have a pull string knob that hangs from a cam on the track, the purpose of which is to disengage the drive motor from the track. With the drive motor engaged, the door is pretty securely locked and it is hard to crank the door up, but not impossible with a jack. Criminals have become extremely specialized at squeezing a coat hanger  through the joints of the garage door and grabbing this knob, hooking it and pulling it downwards, which disengages the drive motor. This is especially made easy when the garage door has glass panels to see within. They can then roll the door up with ease, and by hand. Within the garage, they can then shut the door, and proceed to work on the door to the home with relative privacy. Do yourself a favor and get rid of this pull string and knob altogether. If you really want security, get bicycle wheel lock with the flexible arm, and padlock one of the garage door wheel axles to the track. Most tracks are perforated with holes every few inches, and the wheel axles are easy to grab. This will keep the door in securely locked in the down position.

The Walls

Doors locked? Check. Windows locked? Check. We're safe, right? Well, kind of....not. Have you ever thought about the walls in your home? Consider a crack house for an instant. Usually, it's characterized by extremely heavily fortified doors and windows; so much so that SWAT teams seldom try raiding them by using said doors or windows. In fact, the common tactic in this case is to *saw through the wall with a chain saw*. Structurally speaking, the walls of your home are some of the weakest parts of the house.

In most parts of the country, wood frame construction rules the land. Usually, this means that the walls of the home are 2x6 lumber spaced 16" apart on centers. In really shoddy construction, these can even be 2x4 studs, believe it or not. On the outside of this frame would normally be quarter or three eighths inch plywood (chip board on a shoddy build), some tar paper, and perhaps wood or aluminum siding. Inside, a sheet of ½" drywall. 5/8" if you're lucky.

If you've been doing the math so far, the outside walls of your wood frame home are, at a maximum, 8" thick, and in some tract homes, far thinner. Additionally, most of the wall construction is *air*; you only have a stud every 16"!

Not only is making an entry through a wall easy, it's downright trivial. The chainsaws used to accomplish this are made for cutting down *solid* trees, and have no problem with household walls, which are mostly airspace. By the time you hear the chainsaw start, you have *less than a minute* before armed goons are stomping around in your house.

There is an excellent way of defeating this, however, but it might cost you a few dollars to do it. Here are some methods we like:

- Next time you replace your siding, nail or staple some heavy wire mesh to the entire outside of the home, and then put the siding on overtop. The wire mesh will eat chainsaw blades and give you tons of time to react to what is going on. This mesh is normally sold for concrete applications where it's used to strengthen concrete.

- If you are going to put mesh on your outside walls, consider putting an inch of stucco on the outside walls as well. Not only is stucco long lasting, pretty to look at, and relatively inexpensive, it also offers limited ballistic protection and is very hard to cut through with a chain saw.

- Stone facing is another option we like. It's pricier, but lasts the lifetime of the home and is applied with thin set cement. It affords pretty good ballistic protection from handgun rounds, and it disrupts the trajectory of rifle rounds nicely. Chainsaws can't cut through it!

Vehicle Borne Threats

Many people fail to consider the threat of invasion by vehicle when securing their home. It works kind of like this: Instead of trying to make entry by knocking your door or window out, crooks (even SWAT team members) will basically drive their car into the side of your home or your front door, collapsing the wall in the process, and then charge in through the open hole.

Unless your home is a concrete bunker, it's very difficult to prevent these attacks from a structural standpoint. As discussed previously, wood framed homes are inherently weak, and brick homes aren't well suited to preventing these types of attacks either – the brick just crumbles. There is a solution, however; you may have seen it outside of federal buildings – vehicle countermeasures such as bollards and retaining walls. Bollards are usually

steel pipe sunken into the ground and filled with concrete, or sometimes made of concrete with rebar reinforcement within. Usually, the bollards are arranged so there is enough space for a person to pass through, but not a car, and they are quite resistant to even high-speed vehicle strikes.

Not many homes, however, can adequately place plain bollards on the property and have them look as if they belong. Usually, they need to be disguised as lampposts, plant holders – even statues. Make sure that the bollard has a footing at least one third as deep as it is tall, and if made with cinder block, make sure the cells of the cinderblock are filled with cement and the center is filled with cement and rebar.

Take a look at the driveway to your home. Imagine a truck hurtling towards your front door, and then place obstacles such that they would block the access to that vehicle. Even another car helps protect the home from a charging truck, so if your layout allows it, *park your car in front of your front door!* If your front door is not in the driveway, then make sure the path leading to it has dirt filled planters (steps are better) lining the walkway. Here's a hint – concrete planters can even be sunk in more concrete to fix them in place, so that they act like bollards and prevent someone from driving up on your lawn and ramming your front door. Even a mail box post works as a great bollard – make sure it is filled with concrete and has a solid footing, and then place the mailbox on it. No one will ever know!

What Happens If There Is A Fire?

For this reason, we never recommend metal bars on windows. Even with the 3M window film, the windows work the same as they did before the film. The doors in your house will open with just a few more minor steps, which you will quickly master after opening and closing your new locks a few times. So what about if you somehow pass out and the fire department can't get in? Rest assured, the fire department can always get in. between halligan tools, chainsaws, and hydraulic jaws, and there is nothing that can't be accessed by a team of motivated firemen with enough time. Your fortifications are there to *deter* and *delay* entry, not prevent it outright. First responders will be delayed in getting in to your home, but they will enter. Remember, all you want is a delay so you can arm up if need be!

The Earlier The Better —
Warnings, That Is

Clearly, the theme we've presented when hardening your home is one of *buying time*. If you can just buy yourself a little time when an intruder (or invader) presents himself, you can then take corrective measures such

as arming yourself, calling police, escaping, or anything else you might deem proper at the time. If you aren't given those precious minutes, you get to be a victim and go along with whatever program your intruder has in mind. Not a happy proposition.

EARLY WARNING

It's logical to think then that the more time you buy yourself, the more options you will have. Thus, if you can detect a threat at the perimeter of your property rather than the front door, you will buy yourself that much more time. To that end, there are lots of little gadgets that can help you accomplish this goal.

The one we like best is marketed just about everywhere as a *driveway alarm*. You already know what this gadget is; you just haven't seen it used in this manner before. Walk into any convenience store or gas station, and you will hear a chime as you walk in the door. That little ding-dong tells the clerk or attendant that there is a customer in the store. A little motion detector triggers it, and sounds on a normal speaker somewhere the staff can hear it.

A driveway alarm is the same gadget in a weatherproof housing. We bought and tested a unit off Amazon.com that was under $50. It has a weatherproof motion beam sensor that takes batteries, so there is no wiring whatsoever. Screw the motion beam sensor somewhere solid, and away you go. Oh, and the sensor connects with a control panel inside the home wirelessly, with over a hundred foot range. Whenever the beam is broken in the driveway, the control panel sounds a chime inside. Here are the benefits:

- The driveway alarm is on guard 24 hours per day, and never needs to sleep or be monitored. Whenever someone crosses your predesignated invisible line, the alarm sounds.

- It's a silent alarm, at least to the intruder, meaning you will be well prepared for him when he arrives.

- The sensors can be positioned at a height that will rule out pets, birds, and other nuisance alarms. Set the sensor height at about four feet; not many animals are that tall, but most humans are!

- The sensor beam is invisible to anyone not wearing night vision equipment. The beam is visible with night vision goggles, but not many people have those.

Smile, You're On Camera

In and of themselves, we are lukewarm on surveillance system cameras. This is because you need to be *actually watching* them to detect a threat. A camera does no good if no one is watching the feed; it needs a person to react to what is seen on the screen to work. Of course prisons, shopping malls, and other high security areas have manned camera rooms where actual people are watching the feeds and can radio in if trouble is seen.

At home, cameras make the most sense when they are paired with some sort of alarm system. The simplest of course, is a doorbell – when the bell rings, you glance at the camera feed to see who's there. Think of  it as a high tech peephole. Even better, however, is the pairing of a camera system with a driveway alarm. Most driveway alarms can have up to four sensors, meaning that if one of the sensors goes off and sounds an audible alarm within the home, you can quickly flip to that camera and see what's going on. This is super advantageous because:

- You actually have a way of looking to see *what* tripped the driveway alarm.

- You can visually verify if the alarm is a nuisance alarm such as a pet, the wind, or something else causing a false alarm.

- If your zones are set up correctly with your driveway alarm, you almost never need to watch your camera feeds unless there is an alarm. This means during high threat times (civil unrest, looting), you don't have to man the camera displays and stay awake watching for intruders. Simply let the driveway  alarm do its job, and when it sounds, check the camera feeds and see what caused it.

To Record or Not To Record

Some inexpensive home surveillance camera kits don't come with recording or storage devices. This is fine, assuming you are retired or work from home, and that you are mostly at home during the day and night. However, if you are at work most of the day or travel frequently, a recording camera system with a hard drive for storage makes lots of sense. For starters, you can scrub through the footage and see what happened at your home during the day. This might reveal unsavory visitors who are trying to case the place and check it out while you aren't home. Even if you are home most of the time, you still need to sleep and recording cameras fill you in on the action while you were snoozing. Some tips to think of when purchasing and installing a camera system are:

- Make sure the cameras you purchase have relatively wide-angle lenses.

- Make sure the cameras are weatherproof and above all, have night vision.

- Install the cameras so that they are disguised or partially hidden. A visible camera system becomes a target for an intruder to disable or avoid. You want to catch people in the act, not have them disable the cameras and carry on.

- Get the highest resolution color and HD cameras you can afford. Cheap cameras have grainy images – remember, you might be supplying some of these images to the police to help identify a suspect!

- The biggest point to remember is to make sure the camera views overlap each other in critical areas (like your front door) so that an intruder can't try to hide from the camera, and so when he passes from one camera's field of vision, he gets picked up by another camera.

Safe Rooms: The Final Frontier

Everything we've spoken of up to this point has been how to make your home secure *enough*, or secure within the context of a normal home. The theme which we have presented is one of what you need to do to achieve the minimum level of security required to defeat the average intruder, perhaps the average SWAT call. We are giving you, the prepper, a way to buy time so that you can properly react to the threat at hand, and not immediately fall victim to it. Do what we tell you in this guide, and you can be assured that you will not only be ready for a threat when it emerges, but you will take the element of surprise your aggressor possesses, and flip it around, because in fact <u>your aggressor will be surprised</u> that you anticipated the attack.

But what do you do when facing a determined attacker, someone (perhaps multiple people) who are trying to enter your home and do you harm? What if these people aren't deterred by heavy-duty doors or ballistic window film? What if their idea of a home invasion is to drive a D9 Caterpillar bulldozer into your home, making a 10-foot hole in the wall? When faced with such a determined attack, the only true defense is a *safe room*.

A safe room (or panic room, as depicted in the block-buster movie of the same name) is a fortification built within your home that is designed to thwart a determined attacker. Safe rooms are often reinforced concrete bunkers thinly

disguised as rooms, and are equipped with heavy, safe-style doors. Within the room are communications equipment, weapons, and provisions to keep you alive during the fiercest home invasion.

There are only two objects to safe rooms – money, and your imagination. A safe room can be built in any home, most condos, and even most apartments – if you can pull it off. Here are some of the best design features of safe rooms; keep in mind that your home's layout will dictate what you can actually do:

- The best safe rooms aren't located within the home at all, but they are on the property, usually connected by a tunnel. This is the least feasible but most favorable design.

- Safe room walls should be made of at least 8" of reinforced concrete (containing rebar). Consider that any walk in closet can have walls formed out of concrete and covered in drywall. Just because it is a bunker, doesn't mean it has to look like one!

- Safe room doors should be a vault type, and fireproof. These can be covered over in wood to appear to be normal doors, at least when closed. Even a bank vault door can swing by just the push of a finger on its precise hinges.

- Because safe rooms are usually made of reinforced concrete, they are thus usually located on the ground floor (when the home has no basement), or the basement (when there is no floor beneath). The room physically heavy, and thus must be located on grade.

- All safe rooms should have at least one method of egress besides the front door. Safe rooms are not the Alamo – you don't want to die there. Make sure yours has a method of escape.

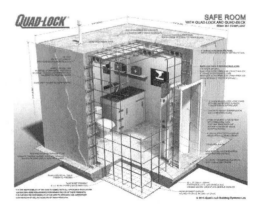

Bulletproof Home Security System

- Safe rooms should contain either a landline connected phone, or a cell booster to facilitate communication. Your radios and cell phones will probably not work inside the safe room unless you have external antennas.

- A great place for a camera display bank is within a safe room! When you are locked inside your safe room, you need eyes and ears – cameras with audio capability are it!

- Equip your safe room with food, water, and defensive weapons. You might be in there for a while!

- The best locks for safe room doors are keyless locks with biometric scan, so they can only be opened by you or someone else who is authorized. Any lock can be picked – any lock except biometric locks!

- Consider that someone may actually try to burn your home down to get you out – make sure your safe room has a water spigot for firefighting, and adequate ventilation. Of course, make sure it is sheathed in fireproof drywall.

- Fresh air ventilation is key. Make sure the vents are disguised on the outside.

The Theme Of What We Are Trying To Present

You need to look at your home just like a criminal, thug, intruder, SWAT team member, or any undesirable will look at it. There is an easy way to do this – be a criminal, on your own home of course. Make a fun game of it, and do it in the daytime. Exit your home and lock the door (but keep the keys handy!). Grab your tools and a ladder, and go around your home, trying to break into it. We guarantee you that without much skill, you'll find at least one easy entry point, and on some old houses, maybe more. And consider you're just using low impact methods (hopefully), rather than outright smashing or destroying. Take what you learn, and fortify, fortify, fortify. Your home is your castle – start treating it like one!

I hope you've enjoyed not only reading this. But, reading is one thing and doing is another. Put these simple steps into action and you'll sleep better at night, I know I do.

And when you have a moment head over to www.FamilySurvival.com and check out everything else we have for you there...